SUPER
BRAIN
TWISTERS

TEST◇YOUR
INTELLIGENCE

SUPER
BRAIN
TWISTERS

NORMAN
SULLIVAN

WARD LOCK

A WARD LOCK BOOK

First published in the UK
1993 by Ward Lock
A Cassell Imprint
Villiers House
41/47 Strand
London
WC2N 5JE

Distributed in the United States by Sterling Publishing Co., Inc.
387 Park Avenue South, New York, New York 10016-8810

Distributed in Australia by Capricorn Link (Australia) Pty Ltd
P.O. Box 665, Lane Cove, NSW 2066

British Library Cataloguing-in-Publication Data
A catalogue record for this book is available from the British Library

ISBN 0-7063-7198-4

Typesetting and design Malca Schotten, illustrations Ruth Rudd

Printed and bound in Great Britain by Cox & Wyman Ltd, Reading

Contents

Read This First 7

Read This First

The *Concise Oxford Dictionary* offers the following definitions: aptitude – natural propensity; intellect – faculty of knowing and reasoning; and intelligence – quickness of understanding. Although these words describe similar characteristics, they are not entirely synonymous, and there are nuances between them that are worth considering.

Most people have a natural aptitude for at least one subject, although they may claim to have no outstanding ability beyond that. An expert in electronics may be completely ignorant about music, or indeed about any other subject outside his or her personal predilection. This innate aptitude for one particular subject is not necessarily evidence of intellect or of intelligence as defined above.

A person with intellect – that is, the ability to reason in subjects other than those for which an outstanding aptitude is possessed – does not have to rely solely on individual preferences. If 'intellect', by definition, means the ability to reason, 'intelligence' goes beyond this and implies an ability to reason quickly. The reason for this distinction is that with intellect one would probably arrive at a solution to a problem if given enough time; an 'intelligent' person, however, would solve the problem in a shorter time.

How, then, can it be possible to assess or improve

these various talents in a book such as this? Certainly the presence or otherwise of aptitude could be verified by confining problems to the one special subject in which the candidate is thought to be proficient, and there is no doubt that aptitude tests are extremely useful in employment selection, for example, when an applicant's suitability for a particular job can be realistically assessed. In itself, however, that would hardly be convincing evidence of either intellect or intelligence. At the same time, objective tests as seen in print are limited in the number of faculties they can cover. Motor skills, which demand manual dexterity, artistic talents or any subject relying on visual, aural or oral contact, can be judged only by seeing or listening to the candidate.

It is generally agreed that objective tests designed to assess a wide variety of abilities should include a reasonable number of questions covering numeracy; verbal skills; the ability to discriminate among similar items; the ability to arrange shapes, words and numbers in a logical order; and the ability to deduce a logical solution from data provided.

In this respect it is the problem-setter's responsibility to ensure that the solution lies within the scope of those being tested and that questions are valid and unambiguous once the root of the problem is discovered.Like a clue in a well-devised cryptic crossword puzzle, the answer should be recognizably valid, however shrouded in obscurity the compiler has made it. At the same time, if the problems are too easy they will hardly give evidence of anything but basic ability and at best could serve as only an indication of elementary 'intelligence'.

Whatever the problem and in whatever subject, in the vast majority of cases success depends on deduction, and it is worth considering that in its own right. Referring to *The Reader's Digest Universal Dictionary* we find that the word 'deduction' is defined as: 'the ability to reach a conclusion by reasoning; the process of reasoning in which *a conclusion follows necessarily from the stated premises*, and logic is a conclusion reached by this process' [my italics]. The only proviso is that the 'stated premises' must give some indication of the lines of reasoning to follow that will lead to the conclusion, and in intelligence tests it is a necessary condition that problems conform to this principle – however adumbrated that conformation may be. And the more difficult the problem, the more obscure this may be.

In most problems it is first necessary to discover the motive that prompted the problem-setter, and this may involve either 'positive thinking' or 'lateral thinking'. A. Heim, an eminent writer on the subject, offers a very apt definition of intelligence: 'the ability to respond the most appropriately *in any given situation* [my italics] and grasp and respond to the essentials in situations which baffle others.'

How true! I have consistently found, in pre-testing

others with these problems, that one person will admit complete defeat or deny any understanding of the meaning of the problems, while another person will hit on the solution almost immediately – even claiming that it is too easy! Nor does this reaction necessarily reflect on the academic status of the person, for intelligence is not solely dependent on education.

Probably the greatest fictional expert in the art of deduction was Sherlock Holmes who, on offering the solution to a problem, would murmur that it was 'elementary'. Elementary to him, no doubt, but it left his colleague, Doctor Watson, completely baffled. And we presume Doctor Watson was no stooge, even though he was portrayed as such in many films.

In these tests the solution to most problems will come from deduction: in numerical problems from deducing the relationship between one number (or set of numbers) and another; in verbal questions from deducing the factor shared by different words. But perhaps the strongest call for deduction will come from deciphering codes and from recognizing the 'stated premises' in the pictorial problems.

Before it became possible to transmit spoken words with or without the medium of wires (as in the case of the telephone, radio or television), it was possible to transmit electrical impulses through wires (telegraphy), and it fell to Samuel Morse over 150 years ago to devise a code by which these impulses could be translated into letters, and from letters into words. Before being able to communicate by this method it was necessary for both sender and receiver to be able to decode the message, and to do this it was necessary to learn the Morse code. In the somewhat elementary decoding problems in this book it is first necessary to master the code, and I have ensured that this should be well within the average reader's ability.

In some of the pictorial problems I have departed from the usual procedure in which pictures have to be matched according to their obvious relationship and have put the emphasis more on deduction, so that you must first translate the pictures into words and then infer the relationship between them. At first sight it will appear there is no connection between any of them and then, when you realize that there *is* a connection, you will have to make a choice from alternatives. A wrong choice with any one pair would lead you astray with other pairs. However, if you examine the pictures carefully you will find at least one pair that forms an obvious match, and this in turn will eliminate alternative possibilities.

Some problems – such as the pictorial ones mentioned above – will plainly take longer to solve than others, just as the solutions to many will strike you at first sight. In addition, some will involve more writing than others, although in almost every answer it is necessary only to write a single letter or number.

To account for these considerations and (more significantly) to encourage quick thinking (remember the definition of 'intelligence'), time limits have been imposed for each test. These time limits take into account the amount of writing involved and the complexity or simplicity of the problems, although, in the case of writing, full allowance has been made for those who write slowly.

You should note the time when you start each test and stop as soon as the time limit is reached, even if you have not completed all the problems. This is because ratings are shown at the end of each group of tests against which you can assess your own performance. For this reason you must keep a record of your score after you have checked the answers, which follow each test. By all means, attempt any unfinished problems, but record only your scores achieved within the time limits.

Should you score full marks in any test you may add one further point to your score.

Start each test with writing materials (both to write your answers and to record your scores) and a clock or watch to check on your start and finish. It does not matter if you have to break off to attend to other matters before the time limit is reached, as long as you note the time when you stop and use the remaining time when you resume.

Each test consists of 15 questions, and they are arranged in three groups:

Group I Easy (four tests)
Group II More difficult (three tests)
Group III Difficult (three tests).

Just as you should check your answers at the end of each test, so you should check your rating at the end of each group, comparing your score with the ratings that follow each group. Reminders to do so are given throughout the book.

What some might regard as a fallacy in the assessment of intelligence by the attainment of high marks in my books on the subject or in similar tests in other publications is the indisputable fact that the more of these tests you do, the better you become at them.There can be no doubt that doing tests of this kind does give an advantage, just as continually solving crossword puzzles in one particular newspaper induces a rapport between reader and compiler, and just as continual activity in any athletic sport can reasonably be expected to bring about improvement.

The age at which this improvement starts going into decline depends largely upon whether there is mental or physical involvement. The muscles, joints, bones – everything that makes for physical development – deteriorate much earlier in life than brain cells, which are responsible for thought processes. It is held that intelligence is related to the number of cells contained in the brain.

However let us leave this proselytizing. I know you are anxious to get started on the tests, but must end by mentioning one further point.

I offer this book in the hope that it will provide many hours of pleasurable and enlightening entertainment. It makes no claim to labelling you with an IQ grading, and I would prefer that it be accepted purely for its value as a form of mental exercise and constructive diversion. If you attain a high rating compared with the ratings given at the end of the book, you have every good reason to be pleased with your efforts; if your rating is below average, don't be down-hearted. It may simply be because you have not encountered objective tests before and that you have failed to grasp the way of going about solving these problems. A low rating is is no evidence that you are in any way inferior mentally to your fellows; indeed, in your own particular field you probably excel, but as the subjects covered in this book do not extend to your own talents you have no way of comparing yourself with others. If you attempt further tests of this nature you will doubtless improve as you come to terms with them.

Many readers will prefer to treat this book as an ordinary puzzle book, just as they would a crossword puzzle book. If you wish to work through the tests without any desire to restrict yourself to the time limits, that is your own prerogative.

However you go about it, I hope you will enjoy pitting your wits, and wish you good luck as you tackle what follows.

Norman Sullivan

GROUP I
– Easy –

Test 1

1. Eleven posts have been erected in a straight line and on level ground at irregular intervals. Ten are of equal length. Which one is a different length?

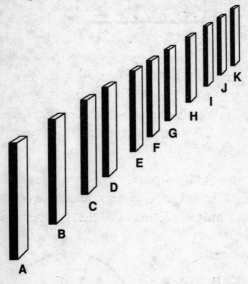

2. From the numbers below and using each number only once in each set, select at least five sets of three that add to 29:

18	6	13	9	19	12
11	4	10	5	8	17

3. Transpose one letter in each of the two words listed below so that two different words result. For example: RIM – SAT becomes RAM – SIT because the I and A have changed places.

    A. SHOW – VIED
    B. STAIN – COVER
    C. DOT – CAM
    D. WASH – CELL
    E. CHAT – WANE
    F. CLOVER – BREACH

4. Four different words can be formed in the first circle and six in the second circle by inserting different letters into the blank sector, reading in either direction. The letters in the sectors should remain in the given order.

    A. What are the ten words?
    B. From the letters used to complete the words, what is the **only** six-letter word that can be made?

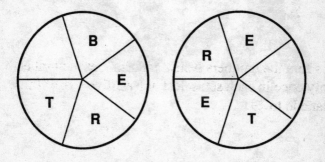

5. Which is the odd one out?

    A. PAIRS
    B. HASTEN
    C. ARABS
    D. SOLO
    E. BAULK
    F. MORE

6. Which spanner fits the nut?

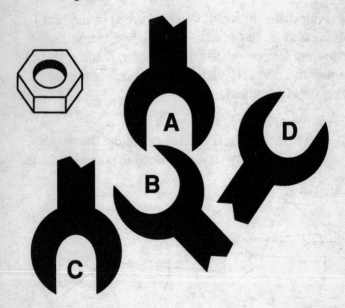

7. Which of the sectors below – A, B, C or D – should fill the empty sector in the circle?

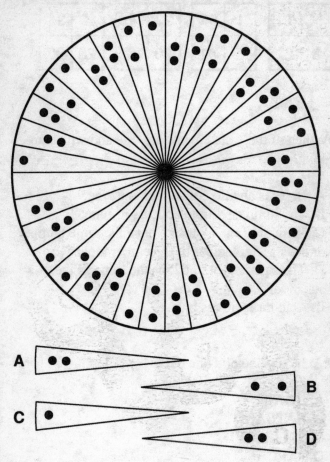

8. What is X?

14	19
8	22

1	50
22	41

22	4
30	8

10	34
28	X

9. Which of these statements are true and which are false?

A. Brass is an alloy of copper and zinc.
B. The summer equinox occurs in June.
C. March to June inclusive have the same number of days as September to December inclusive.
D. The square root of 625 is the same as the square of 5.
E. Acid turns litmus blue.

10. Which is the odd one out?

A. CHAIN
B. HATBAND
C. STELLAR
D. FARCE
E. NOISE

11. What goes into the empty brackets?

2 (38) 3
4 (1524) 5
6 (3548) 7
8 (   ) 9

12. The opposite faces of a die add to seven. The dice below rotate in the directions indicated, one face at a time. After three moves, what will be total of the front faces?

13. A sheet of paper is folded in half and cuts made into it. The paper is then unfolded to reveal this shape. Which of the figures – A, B, C or D – shows the original cuts?

14. In the game of snooker a player must pot a red ball each time before potting a 'coloured' ball (that is, a ball other than red). Each red ball scores 1 point; the 'colours' score as follows:

> Yellow 2
> Green 3
> Brown 4
> Blue 5
> Pink 6
> Black 7

If a player potted two blacks, one yellow, one blue and then two brown balls, followed by one red ball, what would the score be?

15. How many diamonds are there here?

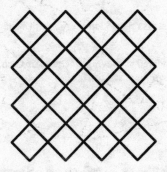

NOW CHECK YOUR ANSWERS
AND KEEP A NOTE OF YOUR SCORE.

Answers

1. K, which is longer (**Score 1 point**)

2. 6+10+13, 8+9+12, 5+6+18, 4+12+13, 8+10+11, 19+4+6, 11+6+12. (**Score 1 point if five or more correct**)

3. A. SHOD–VIEW; B. STAIR–COVEN; C. COT–DAM; D. CASH–WELL; E. WHAT–CANE; F. CLEVER–BROACH. (**Score 1 point if all correct**)

4. A. In the first circle the words are REBUT, TUBER, BERTH, BITER. In the second circle: EATER, ENTER, ETHER, THERE, ERECT, BERET. B. The letters used are B U H I A N H H C and B. The only six-letter word that can be made is HAUNCH. (**Score 1 point if all correct**)

5. C (**Score 1 point**)

ARABS is an anagram of BASRA, which is Iraq's only port, but not its capital. All the others are anagrams of capital cities: A. PARIS; B. ATHENS; D. OSLO; E. KABUL; F. ROME.

6. D (**Score 1 point**)

B is too big; A and C are too small.

7. B (**Score 1 point**)

The position of the spots is repeated in every fourth sector.

8. 87 (**Score 1 point**)

The numbers are considered as moving clockwise in each successive large square. In each case they add to 100:

14 – 50 – 8 – 28

19 – 41 – 30 – 10

22 – 22 – 22 – 34

8 – 1 – 4 – 87 (X)

9. A, C and D are true; B and E are false (**Score 1 point if all correct**)

The summer solstice occurs about 21 or 22 June in the northern hemisphere. Acid turns litmus red.

10 C (**Score 1 point**)

Combine the first two letters with the last two letters: A. CHIN; B. HAND; D. FACE; E. NOSE. If C is treated in the same way, it becomes STAR.

11. 6380 (Score 1 point)

The numbers inside the brackets are the squares of the numbers outside the brackets with 1 deducted. Alternatively, multiply 2, 4, 6 and 8 by 4, 6, 8 and 10 respectively and put the number at the end of the figure in the brackets, and multiply 3, 5, 7 and 9 by 1, 3, 5 and 7 respectively and put these numbers first.

12. 12 (Score 1 point)

	First face	Second face	Third face
1st move	1	2	6
2nd move	4	3	2
3rd move	6	5	1

13. B (Score 1 point)

14. 36 (Score 1 point)

The scores are: 1, 7, 1, 7, 1, 2, 1, 5, 1, 4, 1, 4, and 1.

15. 42 (Sore 1 point)

There are 5 diamonds made with 9 squares, 12 diamonds made with 4 squares, and 25 diamonds made with 1 square.

REMEMBER TO KEEP A NOTE OF YOUR SCORE.

Notes: The most time-consuming questions were probably 4, 8, 12 and 15. In Question 4 you may have missed BERTH in the first circle and THERE and ERECT in the second circle. The anagrams in Question 5 were fairly easy, although the fact that Basra is a port and not a capital city may have caught you out. Question 8 called for lateral thinking; it was easy if you realized that the numbers followed a definable pattern throughout. Question 12 was probably considered the most difficult, and you may have failed to count all the diamonds in Question 15, especially those consisting of nine squares.

Test 2

1. Without inverting the page, how many of these characters will show **different** letters in the same type when turned upside-down?

2. If a pack of playing cards measures 1.3cm when viewed sideways, what would be the measurement if all the aces were removed?

1.3cm

3. Match these designs into six pairs.

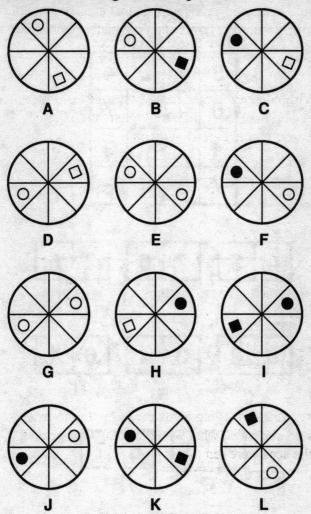

4. Which of the pairs of numbers at the bottom should be placed at X and Y so that each row of four numbers – across, down and diagonally – totals 20?

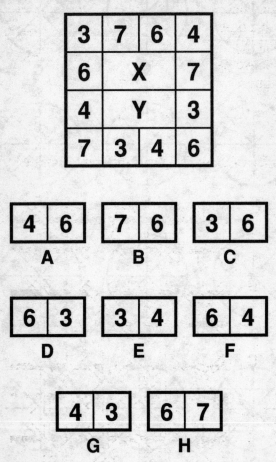

3	7	6	4
6		X		7
4		Y		3
7	3	4	6

4	6		7	6		3	6
A		**B**		**C**	

6	3		3	4		6	4
D		**E**		**F**	

4	3		6	7
G		**H**	

5. Change BOOT into LACE in seven moves, changing one letter at a time and making genuine words each time.

	B	O	O	T
1.	—	—	—	—
2.	—	—	—	—
3.	—	—	—	—
4.	—	—	—	—
5.	—	—	—	—
6.	—	—	—	—
7.	L	A	C	E

6. Which of these designs is different from the others?

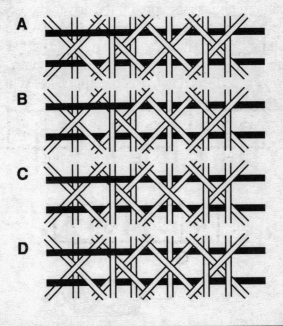

A

B

C

D

7. All of these except one have one thing in common. Which is the odd one out?

   A. 764345896
   B. 125612456
   C. 367874341
   D. 456578325
   E. 178652457
   F. 279651238

8. A feature of many safe-driving competitions consists of a row of poles set at varying distances from each other, ranging from narrow to wide. Maximum points are scored if the driver chooses the narrowest gap through which he can drive without touching a pole. Thus, the driver must relate the width of his car to the width between the poles. Drivers A and B below are competing here. Which gap should each driver choose?

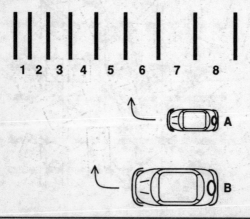

9. Which is the second smallest circle, and which is the second largest circle?

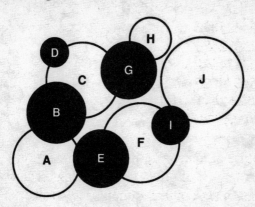

10. Which two dominoes are missing from the set?

11. Which string of beads is the odd one out?

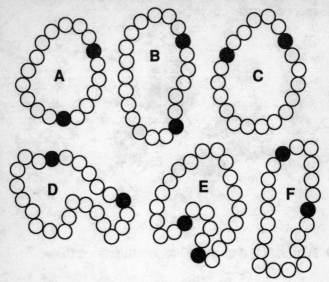

12. What numbers are represented by A, B and C?

A	B	A	B	A	23
B	C	A	A	A	20
B	A	B	C	A	24
B	A	C	C	A	21
B	B	A	A	B	27
31	24	20	21	19

13. Consider these equations and decide which is the odd one out.

A. $6 + 17 - 9 \div 7 + 3$
B. $3 \times 11 + 6 \div 13 + 2$
C. $2 \times 6 \times 3 + 4 \div 10$
D. $1 + 8 - 3 \div 2 + 2$
E. $7 - 4 + 6 - 1 - 3$

14. Which of these designs match each other?

15. What are X and Y?

E O N

O N E

<u>S X Y</u>

**NOW CHECK YOUR ANSWERS
AND KEEP A NOTE OF YOUR SCORE.**

Answers

1. 9 (Score 1 point)

The letters are a b d e g n p q and u.

2. 1.2cm (Score 1 point)

The measurement is reduced by 1/13th (four cards removed from 52).

3. A–D, B–L, C–H, E–G, F–J and I–K (Score 1 point if all correct)

4. X = G, Y = H (Score 1 point)

5. (Score 1 point if all correct. You may score 1 point if you have used other words, as long as they are genuine words)

BOOT: 1. BOUT, 2. TOUT, 3. TAUT, 4. TACT, 5. PACT, 6. PACE, 7. LACE

6. B (Score 1 point)

In the last white cross the diagonal from bottom left to top right should not pass over both vertical slats.

7. E (Score 1 point)

All the others contain three consecutive digits.

8. A. 4, B. 8 (Score 1 point if both correct)

9. I is the second smallest; F is the second largest. (Score 1 point if both correct)

10. 0-0 and 5-2 (Score 1 point if both correct

11. E (Score 1 point)

In E there are four white beads between the two black beads. In the others there are five.

12. A is 3, B is 7, C is 4 (Score 1 point if all correct)

There are several pointers to the solution; for example, in the last vertical column A cannot be 5, 6, 7, 8 or 9.

13. C (Score 1 point)

C results in 4; all the others result in 5.

14. A and F (Score 1 point)

15. X is T, Y is O **(Score 1 point if both correct)**

The letters are the initials of the numbers: E is Eight, O is One, N is Nine, S is Six or Seven, although it must be Six here. Hence:

8 1 9
<u>1 9 8</u>
6 2 1 (subtracting)

REMEMBER TO KEEP A NOTE OF YOUR SCORE.

Notes: The unusual shapes of the characters in Question 1 made it more difficult. Question 4 may have delayed you, as several permutations had to be considered, but Question 9 was easy (too easy, perhaps). Other questions were not very difficult, with the possible exception of Question 15, unless you quickly realized that the letters were the initials of the digits.

---

1. What is the total of the four blank squares in the centre when appropriate numbers are filled in?

1	2	9	1	2	3
8	3	3	4	7	5
4	5			5	6
5	9			4	11
7	8	3	13	8	9
2	15	9	10	1	17

2. Choosing from the words at the bottom, which word should follow those at the top?

MATRIARCH
CHARTER
RETRACE
RECALCITRANT
TRANSEPT

A. PESTILENT
B. PENSIVE
C. TEPID
D. PETROL

3. Which is the odd one out?

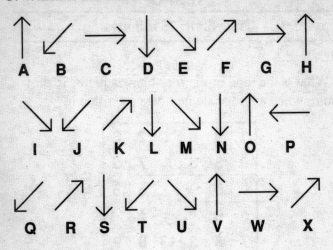

A	B	C	D	E	F	G	H

I	J	K	L	M	N	O	P

Q	R	S	T	U	V	W	X

4. Move each letter one place forwards or backwards in the alphabet to form another word.

FOE

5. What should go into the last line in the left-hand column?

1 8 1 2	9 2 3 4
2 4 2 1	6 4 3 7
1 5 5 6	3 5 7 8
1 4 3 6	2 7 9 4
_ _ _ _	2 5 4 5

6. Which of these contains the greatest number of triangles?

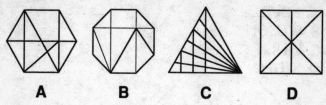

A   **B**   **C**   **D**

7.

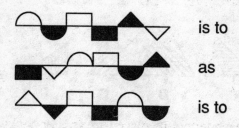

is to

as

is to

Choose from A, B or C.

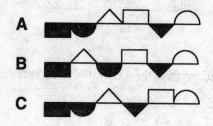

8. What is X?

24 81 63 26 412 8 25x

9. Which row is the odd one out?

A. BDFHJ
B. WUSQN
C. FHJLN
D. KIGEC

10. Which triangle is the odd one out?

11. If 1=X, 2=C and 3=M, what is ½+²⁄₁?

12. If the two spirals at the top are correct, which, if any, of those below are wrong?

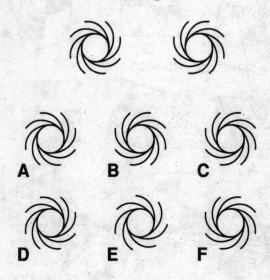

A **B** **C**

D **E** **F**

13. List these words in alphabetical order.

A. BABOON   B. ABBEY
C. CABLE   D. BABY
E. ABACUS   F. CABIN
G. AARDVARK   H. BACON
I. CABAL   J. ABANDON
K. CABBAGE   L. BABYLON

14. Match these patterns into four groups of three and state which is the odd one out.

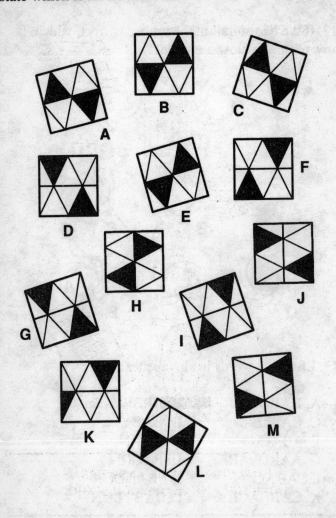

15. Arrange these illustrations into six pairs.

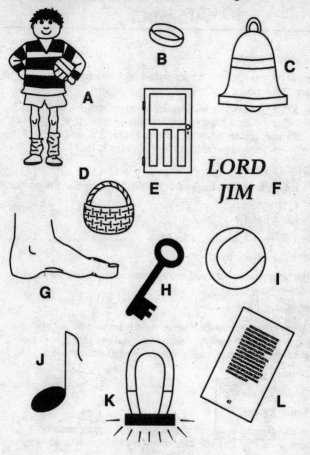

A
B
C
D
E
LORD JIM F
G
H
I
J
K
L

**NOW CHECK YOUR ANSWERS
AND KEEP A NOTE OF YOUR SCORE.**

Answers

1. 26 **(Score 1 point)**

Starting at the top left-hand corner and taking every fourth number, there are four series:

1, 2, 3, 4, 5, 6 (bottom left-hand square in centre section), 7, 8, 9; 2, 3, 4, 5, 6, 7 (bottom right-hand square in centre section), 8, 9, 10; 9, 8, 7, 6 (top left-hand square in centre section), 5, 4, 3, 2, 1; and 1, 3, 5, 7 (top right-hand square in centre section), 9, 11, 13, 15, 17.

2. A **(Score 1 point)**

Each word starts with an anagram of the last four letters of the previous word.

3. P **(Score 1 point)**

It is the only arrow pointing to the left.

4. END **(Score 1 point)**

The first letter moves back; the second letter moves back; the third letter moves back.

5. 1020 **(Score 1 point**

Multiply the first two numbers in the right-hand column and place the result in the left-hand column; multiply the last two numbers in the right-hand column and place the result in the left-hand column.

6. A **(Score 1 point)**

7. A **(Score 1 point)**

8. 6 **(Score 1 point)**

The series is spaced incorrectly. When the spacing is correct it becomes: 2 4 8 16 32 64 128 256, which is an obvious doubling-up series.

9. B **(Score 1 point)**

They are alternate letters of the alphabet. In A they are considered forwards, in B backwards, in C forwards and in D backwards. Therefore, in B the last letter (N) should be O.

10. J (Score 1 point)

It should be the same as C, E and P.

11. 20 (Score 1 point)

X, C and M are the Roman numerals 10, 100 and 1000 respectively. 1000 divided by 100 is 10; 100 divided by 10 is also 10.

12. E (Score 1 point)

There are only seven off-shoots from the centre, instead of eight, as in all the others.

13. G, E, J, B, A, D, L, H, I, K, F and C (Score 1 point if all correct)

14. A–C–H, B–E–L, D–G–M and F–I–J; K is the odd one out (**Score 1 point if all correct**)

15. D–I (basket ball), C–A (bell boy), F–L (title page), G-J (foot note), H–B (key ring) and E–K (door keeper) (**Score 1 point if all correct**)

REMEMBER TO KEEP A NOTE OF YOUR SCORE.

Notes: A more difficult test, although Questions 2, 3, 4, 10, 11, and 13 were fairly easy. The other questions probably made up for this, particularly 1, 6 and 15. In Question 15 boy might have joined with bell, ball or page; door might have joined with bell or key; foot might have joined with ball or note. A wrong choice could have led you astray throughout. If you realized that K was keeper and therefore must have joined with door, this would have narrowed the choice of alternatives.

Test 4

Time limit: 40 minutes

1. Which of the four circles at the bottom should take the place of X?

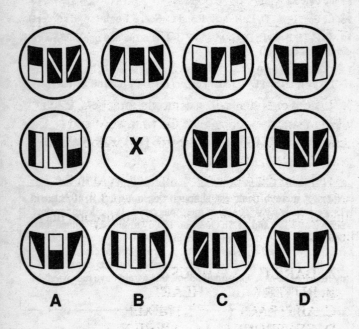

2. Here is part of a menu in a café. What would you expect to pay for a sausage and an egg?

```
.SAUSAGE, EGG & BACON        £1.50
EGG & BACON                  £1.00
SAUSAGE & BACON              80p
```

3. Write words that will go into the brackets. Each word means the opposite of the first word and combines with the second word. For example: BIG (SMALL) HOLDING

Then, taking one letter from each word in the order in which they appear, make a word that means 'the position at which an electrical connection may be made'.

A. DARK (   ) HOUSE
B. BITTER (   ) HEART
C. ABSTRACT (   ) MIXER
D. GENEROUS (   ) WHILE
E. HIT (   ) ION
F. OVER (   ) STAND
G. SLOW (   ) FOOD
H. HATE (   ) LETTER

4. Which cross is wrong?

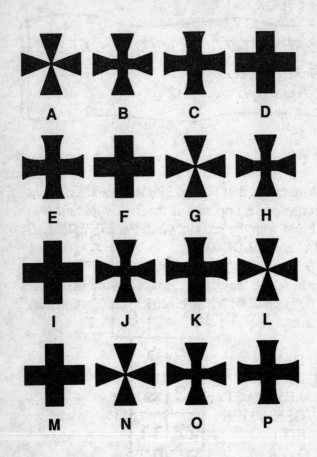

5. Arrange these words in numerical order:
   A. ABRACADABRA
   B. CHALLENGE
   C. MEGALOMANIACAL
   D. CHOPS
   E. ESSENTIAL
   F. MEGALOMANIA
   G. FACET

6. What is X?

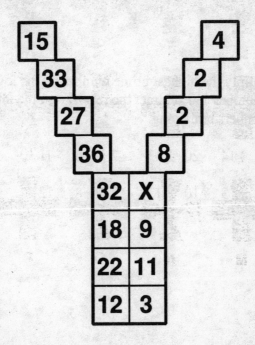

7. Which bar code is wrong?

A   B   C

D   E   F

8. Multiply the highest prime number by the lowest even number and subtract the result from the total of the numbers remaining.

14   20   13   7   16   11

3   10   17   18   8   12

5   6

9. Match these into eight pairs.

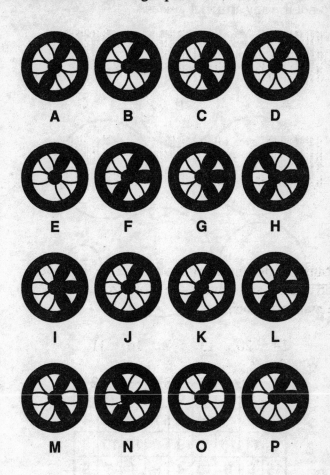

10. Which circle has been drawn by the compass?
(Do not use any artificial guides.)

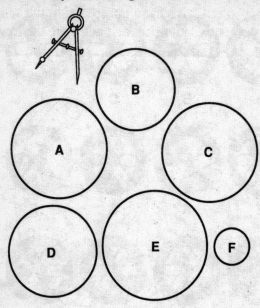

11. What is X?

4	7	9	11	8	15	21	6	5
7	6	1	19	11	7	17	8	4
3	11	15	2	9	8	13	10	9
15	8	3	10	4	9	1	3	9
3	13	10	5	1	10	1	6	19
2	12	11	14	5	6	8	3	X

12. The numbers on a dartboard are arranged as shown below. Add the sum of the 10 consecutive numbers that will give the highest total to the sum of the 10 consecutive numbers that will give the lowest total.

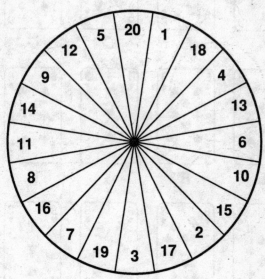

13. Which row is different?

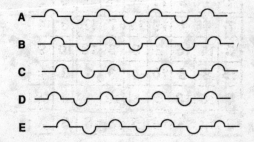

A
B
C
D
E

14. Which is the odd one out?

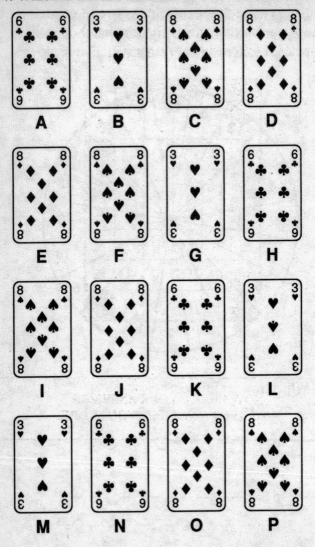

15. Reading across, down or diagonally, and using any letters more than once, find 10 well-known Shakespearean characters. The first letter of each character is printed in heavy type:

**NOW CHECK YOUR ANSWERS
AND KEEP A NOTE OF YOU SCORE.**

Answers

1. C (**Score 1 point**)

The first five patterns indicate that they are globes, rotating anticlockwise.

2. £1.20 (**Score 1 point**)

The menu shows that a sausage costs 50p, an egg, 30p and bacon, 70p

3. A. LIGHT, B. SWEET, C. CONCRETE, D. MEAN, E. MISS, F. UNDER, G. FAST and H. LOVE. The word is TERMINAL. (**Score 1 point if all correct**)

4. K (**Score 1 point**)

It should be like C, E and P.

5. D, G, B, E, A, F and C (**Score 1 point if all correct**)

The order depends on the number of vowels in each word – there is one vowel in CHOPS, but seven in MEGALOMANIACAL.

6. 4 (**Score 1 point**)

The top left-hand number is the result of adding the bottom two numbers. The top right-hand number is the result of dividing the bottom two numbers. If this procedure is followed throughout, X must be 4, to make the top horizontal pair total 36.

7. B (**Score 1 point**)

8. 35 (**Score 1 point**)

The highest prime number is 17, and the lowest even number is 6. The remaining numbers add to 137.

9. A–K, B–P, C–M, D–J, E–O, F–L, G–I and H–N. (**Score 1 point if all correct**)

10. D (**Score 1 point**)

11. 9 (**Score 1 point**)

The numbers under an even number at the top total 30. The numbers under an odd number which is not a prime number at the top total 40. The number under prime numbers at the top total 50.

12. 210 (**Score 1 point**)

The 10 highest numbers (19, 7, 16, 8, 11, 14, 9, 12, 5 and 20) total 121.
The 10 lowest numbers (1, 18, 4, 13, 6, 10, 15, 2, 17 and 3) total 89.

13. E **(Score 1 point)**

Two of the loops are too small.

14. L **(Score 1 point)**

The middle heart has been changed to a spade.

15. Iago, Bottom, Romeo, Othello, Falstaff, Hamlet, Titania, Polonius, Antonio and Orsino. **(Score 1 point if all correct)**

REMEMBER TO KEEP A NOTE OF YOUR SCORE.

Notes: The time limit was generously extended to allow for a considerable amount of writing in Question 12, although a talent for mental arithmetic would save much time. In fact, merely looking at the numbers might have led quickly to the decision that the section containing both 19 and 20 would probably give the highest total (including, as it does, 16, 14, 12 and 11), while the section containing both 1 and 3 would probably produce the lowest total, especially as the intervening numbers also include 2 and 4.

NOW TOTAL YOUR SCORES FOR THE FIRST FOUR TESTS AND COMPARE THEM WITH THE RATINGS THAT FOLLOW.

Ratings in Group I

Test 1 – average 7 points
Test 2 – average 7 points
Test 3 – average 6 points
Test 4 – average 7 points

Out of a possible 60

Over 48	Excellent
39 – 48	Very good
28 – 38	Good
27	Average
22 – 26	Fair
Under 22	Poor

In many cases the division of these problems into groups according to the degree of difficulty has been notional. In any one group there will necessarily be some problems that are relatively easy or difficult within that particular group. The borderline between a 'difficult' problem in an 'easy' group and an 'easy problem in a 'more difficult' group is very narrow. Many of the problems in this group were quite difficult, and some people might claim that they belong to the next group. However, the time limits were more generous than those imposed in our previous books, thus compensating for the greater difficulty. If your score was under 27 it would be advisable to retrace your steps and go right through the tests again, looking especially at the answers and explanations, because it is almost certain that you are not familiar with problems of this nature. Do not lose heart, though, because, as you will discover when you come to the final overall ratings at the end, low scores are more likely than high scores, and the average throughout is well under 50 per cent.

GROUP II
– More Difficult –

Test 1

Time limit: 60 minutes

1. What are A, B, C and D?

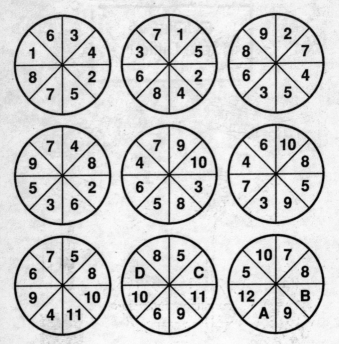

2. What is X?

90 180 12 50 100 200 X 3 50 4 25 2 6 30 3

3. Match these illustrations into eight pairs.

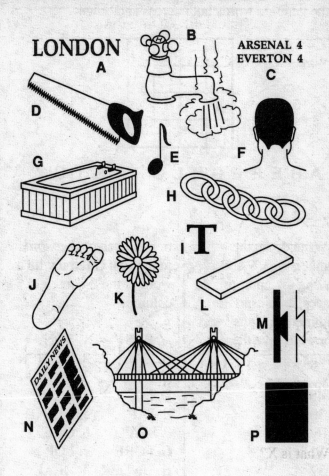

LONDON

A

B

ARSENAL 4
EVERTON 4

C

D

E

F

G

H

I T

J

K

L

M

N

O

P

4. Copy this grid and insert the letters from the list to make genuine words both across and down.

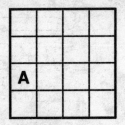

A B E E E G H L O R R S T U Y

5. Write down the numbers 1, 3, 9 and 27, leaving the appropriate spaces, and insert arithmetical signs (+, ×, – or ÷) to give these results.

A. 40
B. 30
C.16
D. 22
E. 39
F. 9
G. 63

6. Pair each of the words in the first column with a word in the second column.

A. REST   1. SON
B. GAL   2. FATHER
C. OR   3. MAN
D. MIS   4. RAIN
E. PAR   5. STAND
F. SEA   6. ORE
G. FORE   7. LOP
H. UNDER   8. DEAL
I. GRAND   9. GO
J. STEP   10. TAKE

7. Which is the odd one out?

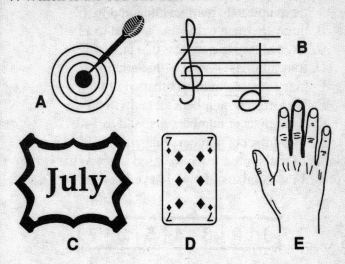

8. In a cricket match five batsmen, A, B, C, D and E, scored an average of 36 runs. D scored 5 more than E; E scored 8 fewer than A; B scored as many as as D and E combined; and B and C scored 107 between them.

How many runs did each man score?

9. In the diagram below you must first eliminate:
   A. three alternate numbers that add to 72
   B. three alternate numbers that add to 114
   C. three alternate numbers that add to 12
   D. four alternate numbers that add to 16
   E. four alternate numbers that add to 64
   F. five adjacent numbers that add to 50
   G. five adjacent numbers that add to 140
   H. five adjacent numbers that add to 190

Some of the numbers may be used twice. What is the total of the numbers that you have not used?

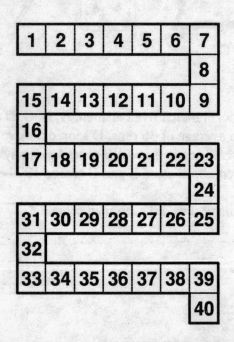

10. If you join all the dots divisible by 3 in ascending order, and then those divisible by 7, also in ascending order, what pattern will result? Use you eye only, and do not use a pointer.

•	•	•	•	•
6	**4**	**18**	**5**	**7**

•	•	•	•	•
1	**22**	**2**	**20**	**8**

•	•	•	•	•
28	**10**	**21**	**11**	**14**

•	•	•	•	•
16	**23**	**13**	**25**	**29**

•	•	•	•	•
35	**17**	**33**	**19**	**39**

11. From the three examples above, decide what goes into the empty brackets below.

635 (53) 714
294 (18) 832
153 (21) 264

742 (   ) 498

12. Change one letter in the first word to form the second word. Definitions are given for each word.

A. The provision of help to the poor – Clearness
B. Exposed – Changed the position of
C. The vane of an arrow – The state of the atmosphere at a given time
D. To despoil – Wild and untamed
E. A Christian festival – To overcome
F. A formation in rugby – The fluid obtained from separating blood into components
G. A fusible alloy – Having a lower temperature
H. A motive – To add flavouring to food
I. A lathe worker – The part of stove that produces a flame
J. To emphasize a printed word – To weaken
K. A group of followers – To hearten
L. The full number to make a crew or staff – expression of praise
M. To eject liquid in a thin stream – An English country gentleman
N. To coagulate – To hide
O. The means of transmission without wires – Proportion

13. What are A, B, C and D in the bottom two circles?

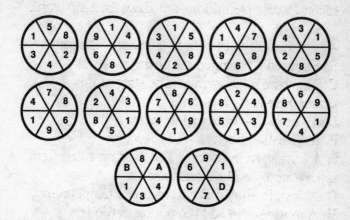

14. What is X?

737   382
461   955
392   745
183   297
468   246
732   58X

15. Which four of the smaller pieces will fit together to complete the map of Britain?

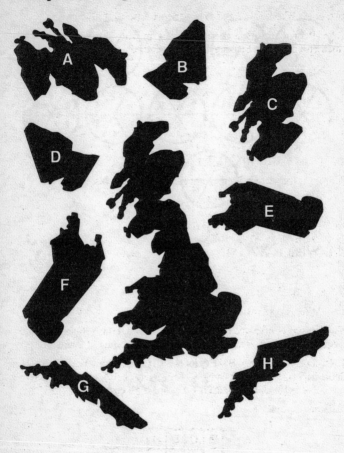

Answers

1. A is 11, B is 6, C is 7 and D is 4 **(Score 1 point if all correct)**

Take alternate sectors in alternate circles, moving always in a clockwise direction. Starting at the first circle:

1	2	3	4	5
6	7	8	9	10
3	4	5	6	7
4	5	6	7	8
2	3	4	5	6 (B)
5	6	7	8	9
7	8	9	10	11 (A)
8	9	10	11	12

Starting at the second circle, and again going clockwise:

3	4	5	6
7	8	9	10
1	2	3	4 (D)
5	6	7	8
2	3	4	5
4	5	6	7 (C)
8	9	10	11
6	7	8	9

2. 150 **(Score 1 point)**

The first term (90) is the product of the last two terms (30 and 3). This procedure is followed throughout, so X is the product of 3 and 50.

3. A – I (Capital letter), B – F (Hot head), C – O (Draw bridge), E – N (Note paper), J – G (Foot bath), K – H (Daisy chain), M – D (Tenon saw), P – L (Black board). **(Score 1 point if all correct)**

4. (Score 1 point)

5 A. 1+3+9+27; B. 1+3x9+27; C. 1-3-9+27; D. 1+3-9+27;
E. 1x3+9+27; F. 1+3x9-27; G. 1+3x9+27. (**Score 1 point if all correct**)

6. A – 4, B – 6, C – 7, D – 8, E – 10, F – 1, G – 3, H – 9, I – 5, J – 2
(**Score 1 point if all correct**).

7. C (**Score 1 point**)

Apart from C, they are all 'middles': A is the bull – or middle – of the target; B is middle C; D is the middle card of that suit; E is the middle finger. July is *not* the middle month of the year.

8. A scored 28 runs; B scored 45 runs; C scored 62 runs; D scored 25 runs; and E scored 20 runs (**Score 1 point if all correct**)

If B and C scored 107, A, D and E must have scored a total of 73 runs. If A scored x runs, x+x-8+5+x-8=73, therefore, 3x=84 so x=28

From knowing that A scored 28 runs it is easy to discover how many the other players scored.

9. 302 (**Score 1 point if all correct**)

A. 22-24-26; B. 36-38-40; C. 2-4-6; D. 1-3-5-7; E. 13-15-17-19;
F. 8-9-10-11-12; G. 26-27-28-29-30; H. 36-37-38-39-40. The numbers not used are 14-16-18-20-21-23-25-31-32-33-34-35.

10. A swastika (**Score 1 point**)

11. 10 (**Score 1 point**)

Add the sum of the digits on either side of the brackets to the sum of the digits in the brackets above. Hence: 7+4+2=13, which, by adding the digits, is 4; 4+9+8=21, which, by adding the digits, is 3; the sum of the digits in the brackets above – 21 – is 3; 4+3+3=10.

12. A. Charity, Clarity; B. Displayed, Displaced; C. Feather, Weather; D. Ravage, Savage; E. Easter, Master; F. Scrum, Serum; G. Solder, Colder; H. Reason, Season; I. Turner, Burner; J. Underline, Undermine; K. Entourage, Encourage; L. Complement, Compliment; M. Squirt, Squire; N. Congeal, Conceal; O. Radio, Ratio (**Score 2 points if all correct; 1 point if 13 or 14 correct**)

13. A is 2, B is 5, C is 8 and D is 4 (**Score 1 point if all correct**)

In alternate circles, starting with the first circle, the numbers advance one sector clockwise; starting with the second circle the numbers go back one sector anticlockwise.

14. 5 (Score 1 point)

The numbers in the horizontal lines add to 30. In the last line the numbers add up to 25, so X must be 5 to bring the total to 30.

15. A, B, F and H (Score 1 point if all correct)

The pieces fit together like this:

REMEMBER TO KEEP A NOTE OF YOUR SCORE.

Notes: In Question 1 the circles interposed between the relevant circles (in alternate positions) are distractors. If you concentrate your attention on the alternate circles, ignoring those in between, the solution becomes apparent. In Question 3 it is very probable that you started by matching A with O, to give London Bridge. This, or any wrong pairing in the early stages, would have led to an unsatisfactory result. In Question 14 you may have elected to add the vertical columns; taking the horizontal lines into consideration may have escaped you – surely a perfect demonstration of lateral thinking!

1. Which is the odd one out?

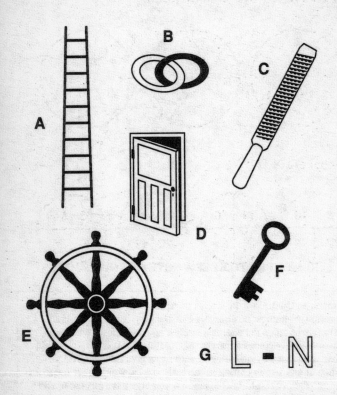

2. The exact position of the hands on these clocks point to whole numbers or fractions of numbers. Thus, the first clock shows a total of 12½ (the minute hand points to 6 and the hour hand to 6½).
Give the total represented by all three clocks. What will the total be in 2½ hours time?

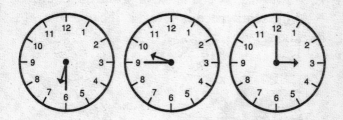

3. What are X and Y?

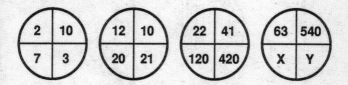

4. Will pinion Y rotate:
   A. Faster than X and in the same direction?
   B. Slower than X and in the same direction?
   C. At the same speed as X and in the same direction?
   D. Faster than X and in the opposite direction?
   E. Slower than X and in the opposite direction?
   F. At the same speed as X and in the opposite direction?

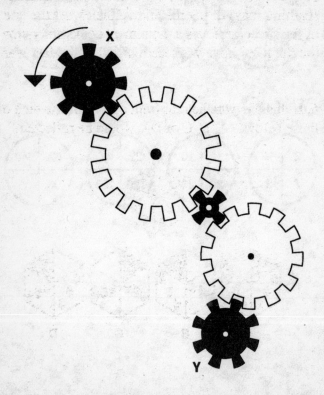

5. How many mistakes can you find here?

In the town their were shops of every discription, but the biggest shop was stocked with such things as lawn mower's and garden tools.

Two shops were managed by Stan and Bert, the son-in-laws of the town counsillor. Stan sold *objects d'art*, while Bert's shop was stocked with electical goods. In the High Street their was a seathing mass of people and vehacles. At the end of the street there was a monument comemmorating the the local boys who were killed in the last war.

6. If this die were held in front of a mirror, which of those below – A, B, C or D – would be reflected?

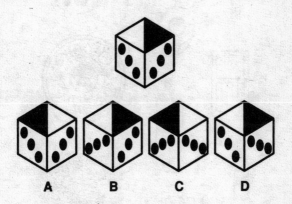

A   B   C   D

7. State the combined total of both these series when you have substituted numbers for X and Y.

2 5 8 11 X 17

1 4 7 4 7 10 7 Y 13 10 13 16 13 16

8. Match these illustrations into six pairs.

9. Here are two months in code:

D B Y E F
B G H G I J

and one day, using the same code:

X Y Z A B C

Now decode this statement from a language teacher:

Z IGHHKIJ JFBJ ZJ ZI YZHFJ ZX
B EFZMA ZI JBGHFJ HNNA
HYBDDBY

10. Take a two-digit number and multiply it by its square root. The result is the same as the square of half the original number. What is the original number?

Then, multiply the answer by four and add the result to double the original number.

11. What are X, Y and Z?

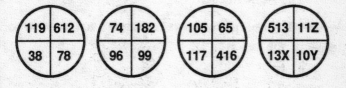

77

12. If ZOO=OUT, and SUP=ROW, what is HATRED?

Choose from these

    A. LOOM
    B. MOTH
    C. PHASED
    D. MARSH

13. When the minute hand points to 9 minutes and the second hand points to 18 seconds the acute angle between them is between:

    A. 30 and 40 degrees
    B. 40 and 50 degrees
    C. 50 and 60 degrees

If clock A shows 8.30 and clock B shows 5.40, is the acute angle between the hands:

    A. Greater in A?
    B. Greater in B?
    C. The same in each?

Which of these times shows the largest acute angle between the hands?

    A. 2.20
    B. 7.25
    C. 8.50

14. A runner, a cyclist and a motorist compete over a 10-mile course. The runner, who averaged 10 mph, started at 1.10 pm. The cyclist, who averaged 12 mph, started at 1.20 pm. The motorist, who could only average 20 mph because of heavy traffic, started at 1.40 pm.

In what order did they finish?

15. Which is the odd one out?

A. The actor mentioned that he wanted a bigger part.
B. The invaders, taking the city by storm, entered the city gates without resistance.
C. A servant or mental case deserves pity.
D. The victor entertained the vanquished.

**NOW CHECK YOUR ANSWERS
AND KEEP A NOTE OF YOUR SCORE.**

Answers

1. F (Score 1 point)

A and C go together (ladder and rasp); D and B go together (open and link); E and G go together (helm and dash). In each case, the first letter is removed, to give: adder and asp (A and C), pen and ink (D and B), and elm and ash (E and G).

2. 46¼, 47¾ (Score 1 point if both correct)

The total now is: 12½ + 18¾ + 15 = 46¼

The total in 2½ hours will be 21 + 15¼ + 11½ = 47¾

3. X is 902, Y is 50400 (Score 1 point if both correct)

In each circle the number in the top left quarter is the sum of the top two quarters in the previous circle; the number in the top right is the sum of the bottom two quarters in the previous circle; the number in the bottom left quarter is the product of the two numbers in the previous circle: the number in the bottom right quarter is the product of the two numbers in the bottom two quarters in the previous circle. therefore, X is the product of 22 and 41; and Y is the product of 120 and 420.

4. C (Score 1 point)

A pinion interposed between two other pinions does not change the ratio between the others, but it does change the direction of rotation. Nor does it matter how many pinions are interposed, but because, in this case, there are three intermediate pinions, the direction of rotation will remain as in the original.

5. 12 (Score 1 point if you found them all)

The mistakes are: there; description; mowers; sons-in-law; councillor; objets d'art; electrical; there; seething; vehicles; commemorating; the (repeated).

6. A (Score 1 point)

7. 188 **(Score 1 point)**

X is 14 and Y is 10 to complete the series. The top series advances each number by 3, so X is 14; the bottom series advances every fourth row by 3, so Y advances 7 (the 5th term) by 3 to become 10.

8. A–H (telephone box), B–K (man Friday), E–D (nut bolt), G–C (door hinge), J–F (shellfish) and L–I (sundial) **(Score 1 point if all correct)**

9. I suggest that it is right if a child is taught good grammar **(Score 1 point)**

The second month is August, the only month with six letters; the first letter, A, indicates that the second letter of the first month must also be A, and therefore that month must be March. It is then obvious that the day must be Friday, since it cannot be Sunday or Monday. Substituting the known letters, it is a straightforward matter to decode the message.

10. 16 and 96 **(Score 1 point if both correct)**

16 multiplied by 4 (its square root) is 64, which is the same as the square of 8 (half of 16). 32 (double 16) added to 64 gives 96.

11. X is 7, Y is 1 and Z is 4 **(Score 1 point if all correct)**

Add the digits in each number and the result is the same in each successive quarter moving clockwise: 119 (11), 182 (11), 416 (11), 137(X) (11); 612 (9), 99 (18 – that is, 9), 513(9); 117 (9), 78 (15 – that is, 6), 96 (15 – that is, 6), 105 (6), 114(Z) (6); 38 (11 – that is, 2), 74 (11 – that is, 2) 65 (11 – that is, 2), 101(Y) (2).

12. B **(Score 1 point)**

Substitute numbers for letters according to their alphabetical position: ZOO (56) = OUT (56); SUP (56) = ROW (56); HATRED (56) = MOTH (56).

13. C, A, B **(Score 1 point if all correct)**

14. They all finished at the same time (2.10pm) **(Score 1 point)**

15. D **(Score 1 point)**

All the others contain the word torment.

REMEMBER TO KEEP A NOTE OF YOUR SCORE.

Notes: The pictures in Question 1 may have seemed to have nothing in common. One method of dealing with all pictorial problems is to begin by writing down what each picture signifies. In this case it may then have become apparent that the initial letter had to be removed from each word. Another pictorial problem, Question 8, had to be treated quite differently. If you paired telephone with dial, or nut with shell, for example, you would have gone adrift later. No great difficulty with Question 9 if you applied simple deduction to the decoding of the months and the day. In previous books I have pointed out that, when you are faced with a problem mixing letters with numbers or variations on that theme, it is worth giving the letters values according to their position in the alphabet (Question 12). The answer to Question 14 was fairly easy, especially if you recognized immediately that the runner, whose speed was 10 mph, must have taken exactly one hour to complete the course.

Test 3

Time limit 60 minutes

1. Which illustration is the odd one out?

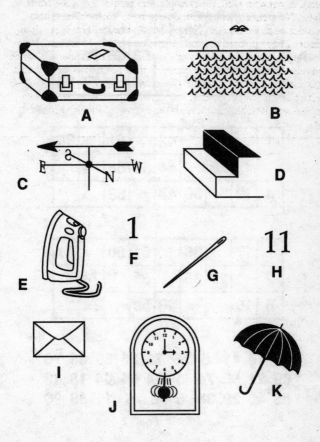

2. Here are three bingo cards. The numbers are called out in the order shown below. Without writing or marking the numbers, which card is the first to get a full line across, and in how many numbers called was the winning line claimed?

A

3			36	41		64	70	
	13	24			53	66	75	
	19		37		58		77	90

B

1		25		42		61		88
		29		44	56	68	71	
4	12		30	48		69		

C

	17		35		51	60		87
2		22	38		55		73	
6	18			40	59		74	

87 16 41 3 59 71 33 50 68 70
89 21 56 74 5 14 64 44 18 43
65 40 29 36 6 8 9 11 88 90

3. If you wanted pinion 2 to rotate twice as fast as pinion 1, which of the pinions below – A , B, C or D – would you mesh between them?

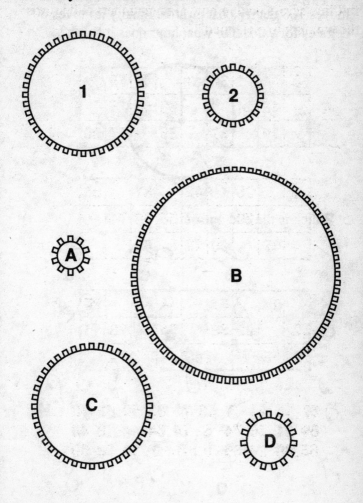

4. This hour hand moves 25 degrees backwards and then it moves 35 degrees forwards. Then it moves to the position diametrically opposite, from which it moves 100 degrees backwards. Finally it moves 60 degrees forwards. On what hour does it finish?

5. Which is the odd one out?

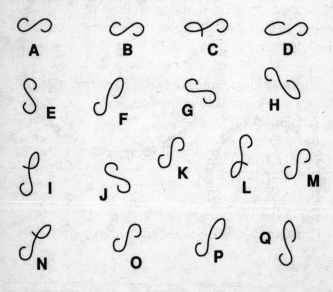

A

B

C

D

E

F

G

H

I

J

K

L

M

N

O

P

Q

6. In this problem you must not use measuring instruments, but you may draw a freehand sketch, endeavouring to keep to fairly correct proportions. From point X, a person walks 50 metres southwest, then 100

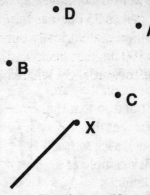

metres east, then 120 metres north, then 50 metres west, followed by 70 metres southeast, 50 metres west, and finally 35 metres northwest.

In the diagram above, decide which spot will be the nearest to the finishing point. Base your proportions on the first leg of the journey, which is already indicated.

7. Which of these words does not have something that the other words have in common?

    A. BEGIN

    B. ACE

    C. MOQUETTE

    D. UNPRIMED

    E. HANDICRAFT

    F. FORCEFUL

    G. BOOKMOBILE (a mobile library)

8. What is X?

6	7	12	11	5	9	13	8	X
2	4	3	9	2	3	6	7	1	2

9. In a normal pack of playing cards some cards look different when they are turned round so that the top appears at the bottom and vice versa, as in this example of a simple letter.

If all the aces and picture cards are removed, there is only one suit that has only one card that looks different when it is turned round. What is the suit? What is the card?

10. A total of 27 loose blocks are placed in the form of a cube. Two of these blocks, indicated by X, are then removed. Which of the blocks A, B, or C will remain?

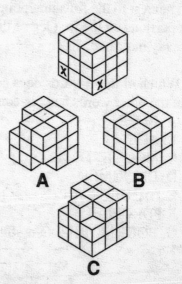

11. Which three of these numbers will add to 1000?

264   136   547   192
756   631   249   233

12. The receptacle at the top is filled with water. If its contents were poured into the six receptacles below, which of them, if any, would overflow?

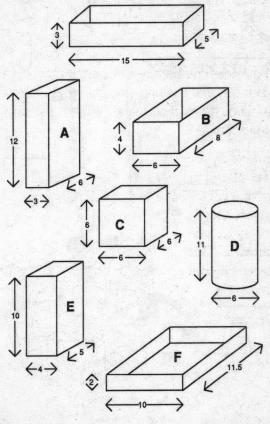

13. Match these illustration into seven pairs.

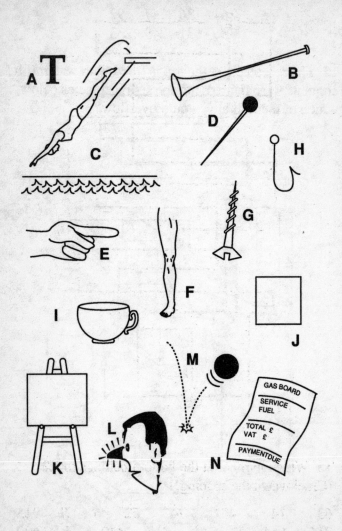

14. Which is the shortest route from A to B?

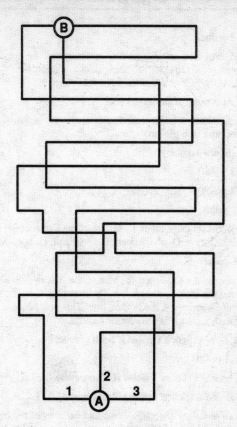

15. Which number at the bottom belongs to X?
(Clue: watch the spacing!)

63	14	431	74	52	6	X	915
716	654	7	14	812	449	11	600

Answers

1. H (Score 1 point)

Apart from H, they all start with the last two letters of the previous word (as shown pictorially): caSE, SEA, EAST, STaIR, IRON, ONE, NEedLE, ELevEN, ENveloPE, PEndulUM, UMbrella.

2. B, 23 (Score 1 point if both correct)

3. Any of them (Score 1 point, but do not score any points if you have specified any one pinion)

4. 5 o'clock (Score 1 point)

5. H (Score 1 point)

6. D (Score 1 point)

7. E (Score 1 point)

All the others contain three alternate letters of the alphabet: A. BEGin; B. ACE; C. MOQuette; D. uNPRimed; F. forCEFul; G. booKMObile.

8. 3 (Score 1 point)

The first number in the top line is the sum of the first two numbers in the bottom line; the next number in the top line is the sum of the second and third numbers in the bottom line. This procedure is followed throughout, so X is the sum of 1 and 2.

9. Diamonds, Seven (Score 1 point if both correct)

10. C (Score 1 point)

11. 136, 631 and 233 (Score 1 point if all correct)

12. A, B, C, D and E (Score 1 point if all correct)

They would all overflow except F. The cubic capacity of the top receptacle is 225 cubic units. The other containers will hold: A. 216, B. 192, C. 216, D. 207 (approximately), and E. 200, cubic units.

13. A–J (T-square), D–E (pinpoint), F–B (leghorn), G–M (screwball), I–K (cupboard), L–C (nosedive) and N–H (billhook). (Score 1 point if all correct)

14. 1 (Score 1 point)

15. 716 **(Score 1 point)**

When it is spaced correctly the top line reads: 631, 443, 174, 526, 716(X), 915. Adding the digits that make up each number: 10, 11, 12, 13, 14, 15.

REMEMBER TO KEEP A NOTE OF YOUR SCORE.

> **Notes:** An extremely difficult test. The pictorial problems in Question 1 departed from the usual pairing system, and you were doubtless trying to match the pictures. I hope, in Question 3, you remembered our previous advice that intermediate pinions do not change the ratio of other pinions. In Question 10 the operative word was 'loose'. Because the blocks were not joined, the removal of any supporting block would cause those above it to fall. In Question 13 much depended on your making a correct choice for the first pair. If, for example, you paired T with cup (instead of square) it would have thrown you out with later pairs. Question 15 would have been too difficult but for the clue.

NOW TOTAL YOUR SCORES FOR THE THREE TESTS IN THIS GROUP AND COMPARE THEM WITH THE RATINGS THAT FOLLOW.

Ratings in Group II

Test 1 – Average 6 points
Test 2 – Average 6 points
Test 3 – Average 7 points

Out of a possible 46

Over 35	Excellent
27–34	Very good
20–26	Good
19	Average
13–18	Fair
Under 13	Poor

The time limits were probably responsible for most of the problems that you failed to solve correctly. Given more time you would probably have succeeded. This was particularly the case in Question 3 in Test 3, in which very little time was allowed for what should have been the obvious answer; if you unnecessarily counted all the teeth on the pinions you would have spent a long time on this one problem.

Questions for which adequate time was allowed to compensate for the amount of writing or working out involved were Questions 1, 2, 5, 7, 9 and 13 in Test 1; Questions 2, 12 and 13 in Test 2; and Questions 1, 8, 12 and 14 in Test 3.

Comparatively low scores were the norm, and if you scored under 13 I can only repeat the advice to go through all the answers and explanations again to gain a better comprehension of these types of tests, especially because you may meet greater difficulties in the next group.

GROUP III
– Difficult –

Test I

Time limit: 50 minutes

1. The total of the three teeth meshed at point A is 6 (3, 2 and 1). The three teeth meshed at B total 28 (5, 11 and 12). When X rotates anti-clockwise to Y, what will be the total of the six teeth meshed at A and B?

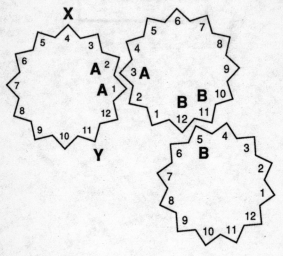

2. There are two points available here. Write words that have opposite meanings to the words in italics, and then take a letter from each word you have chosen to make a word meaning points out.

Although it was a *dark day*, he could see *over* the road. He saw a *poor* man *slowly running*, *giving light* steps, in spite of his *large* feet.

3. Which row is the odd one out?

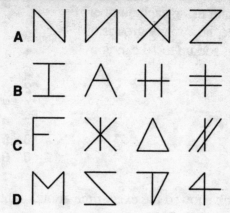

4. Which two make a matching pair?

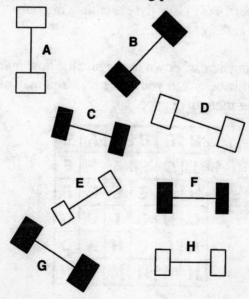

5. Taking one number from each column and using each number only once, how many groups of three that add up to 10 can you find?

1	8	1
6	5	3
9	4	1
3	1	3
5	1	2
2	0	1
4	7	0
7	4	2
0	0	2
8	9	1

6. A clock showed the exact time at midnight on 31 December 1987. If it gained two seconds every day, what time would it have shown at midnight on 31 December 1988? Give the exact time in hours minutes and seconds.

7. Reading across, down or diagonally, how many parts of the body can you find here? You may use any letter more than once.

N	R	E	C	A	L
I	O	S	A	F	E
H	E	E	L	B	F
C	N	G	T	O	O
K	L	E	H	W	D
N	A	R	M	A	N

8. Which is the odd one out?

A. 9 8 6 3 1 4 7
B. 6 1 5 3 2 0 3
C. 4 7 9 0 1 8 2
D. 1 6 7 2 1 0 4
E. 3 2 4 4 2 8 6
F. 4 6 7 3 1 1 2
G. 7 8 8 1 1 9 4

9.

If 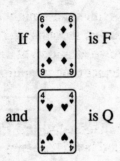 is F

and is Q

what is

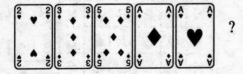 ?

10. What are A, B and C? (There are three clues.)

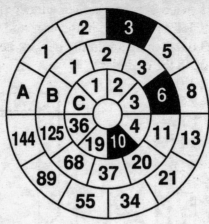

11. What goes into the empty rectangles at the bottom?

	11	3
K	13	5	C
M	4	10	E
D	14	2	J
N	3	6	B
C	1	8	F
A	?	?	H
V			M

12. If 54 balls are placed into the three receptacles, so that there are twice as many in the cylinder and bucket combined as there are in the box, and twice as many in the box as there are in the bucket, how many balls are there in the cylinder?

13. Here are three months represented by numbers:

1 2 3 4 5 6 4 7
8 4 9 4 5 6 4 7
10 4 6 7 11 12 7 13

What words are these?

A. 4 1 9 11 5 6 7 12 1 9 4
B. 9 11 9 11 5 6 4 7

14. Match these strokes into 8 pairs.

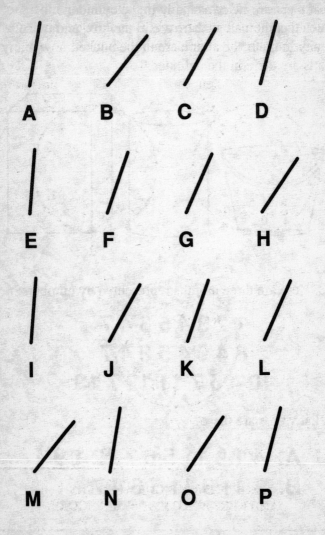

15. This problem is for mental solving only! Do not use a pencil and paper. Add the alternate numbers in A to the alternate numbers in B and divide the result by the sum of the alternate numbers in C.

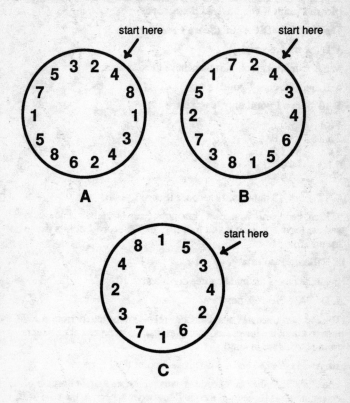

Answers

1. 40 (Score 1 point)

2. light, night, under, rich, quickly, walking, taking, heavy and small
(Score 1 point if you have all these words)

The word is INDICATES **(Score 1 point extra)**

3. D (Score 1 point)

M has four strokes: all the others have three strokes.

4. B and G (Score 1 point)

5. 10 (Score 1 point only if you have 10)

1 8 1	9 0 1
2 5 3	3 7 0
5 4 1	4 4 2
6 1 3	8 0 2
7 1 2	0 9 1

6. 12 hours, 12 minutes, 12 seconds (Score 1 point)

7. Face, hand, arm, foot, calf, chin, nose, heel, leg, elbow, knee, ankle
and ear **(Score 1 point if you found 11 or 12; Score 2 points if you
found 13)**

8. F (Score 1 point)

In all the others the middle three digits add to 10.

9. OCEAN (Score 1 point)

The top card indicates that diamonds represent the letters from A to M
(ace to king); the lower card indicates that hearts represent the letters
from N to Z (ace to king).

10. A=233, B=230 and C=69 (Score 1 point if all correct)

The clues lie in the black sections, which indicate that, in the case of A,
each number is the sum of the previous two numbers; in the case of B,
each number is the sum of the previous three numbers; in the case of C,
each number is the sum of the previous four numbers.

11. | 22 | 13 | (Score 1 point)

The numbers in the upper rectangles correspond with the alphabetical
position of the numbers in the lower rectangles.

12. 27 (Score 1 point)

There are 9 balls in the bucket and 18 balls in the box

13. A. ENCUMBRANCE, B. CUCUMBER (Score 1 point if both correct)

The months are November, December and February.

14. A–N, B–M, C–J, D–P, E–I, F–K, G–L and H–O (Score 1 point if all correct)

15. 5 (Score 1 point)

Alternate numbers in A add to 30; alternate numbers in B add to 40; alternate numbers in C add to 14. 70 divided by 14 is 5.

REMEMBER TO KEEP A NOTE OF YOUR SCORE.

Notes: In Question 1 the numbers are moved seven places, first anticlockwise, then clockwise, and finally anticlockwise again. Much time may have been spent on Questions 5, 7 and 13. Did you remember in Question 6 that 1988 was a leap year, and hence contained 366 days? Question 9 may have stumped you unless you have read my previous books, in which I pointed out that, having hit on the fact that there are 26 cards in two suits and 26 letters in the alphabet I would use this ploy again. I have! Don't be surprised to meet it again! Question 12 was quite easily solved without resorting to algebra. I hope that you solved Question 15 mentally without putting pen to paper.

Test 2

1. Each of four players holds three cards – a jack, queen and king. Player A has all red cards. Player B has all black cards. Player C has two hearts and one black card. Player D has two queens and a king.

   If players C and D exchanged their odd suits D would have all spades. Which player originally held the jack of spades?

2. Low is to high as:
   A. Heavy is to _ _ _ _ _
   B. Happy is to _ _ _
   C. Port is to _ _ _ _ _ _ _ _ _ _
   D. Love is to _ _ _ _
   E. Introvert is to _ _ _ _ _ _ _ _ _
   F. Fact is to _ _ _ _ _ _ _
   G. Loser is to _ _ _ _ _ _
   H. Good is to _ _ _
   I. Waking is to _ _ _ _ _ _ _ _
   J. Piano is to _ _ _ _ _

3. Which is the odd one out?

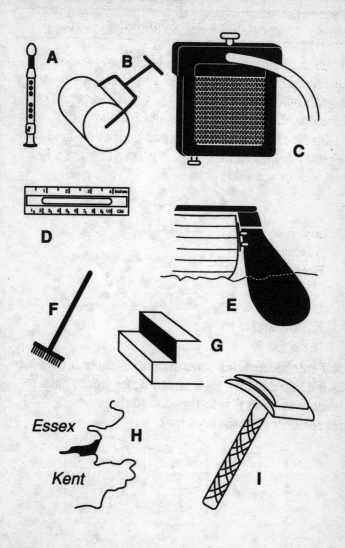

4. In these epicyclic gears, when pinion A completes three revolutions where will the tooth marked X on pinion B be? Choose from A, B, C and D below.

A   **B**   **C**   **D**

5. Three receptacles contain certain amounts of water as indicated below. How much water would have to be poured from A into B and C so that each receptacle contains the same?

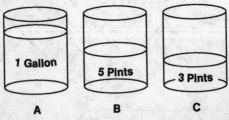

| 1 Gallon | 5 Pints | 3 Pints |

A   **B**   **C**

6. Which is the odd one out?

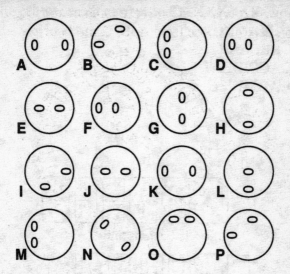

7. What are X, Y and Z?

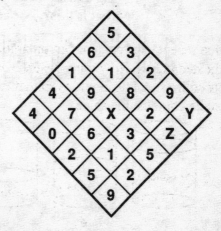

8. If XXXX is ACCENT, and XXXXXXX is ACME, what is: XXXXXX? Choose from these words:
   A. EXAMINE
   B. REDCAP
   C. ACCIDENT
   D. ADMIT

9.

If

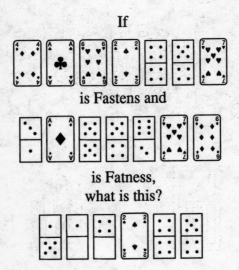

is Fastens and

is Fatness,
what is this?

10. Which is the odd one out?

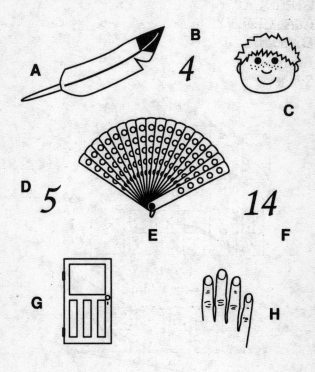

A

B

4

C

D

5

E

F

14

G

H

11. Here is a map of Australia. If you flew direct from Perth to the following towns in the order listed, which of the three routes shown below would you follow?

Adelaide
Melbourne
Brisbane
Sydney

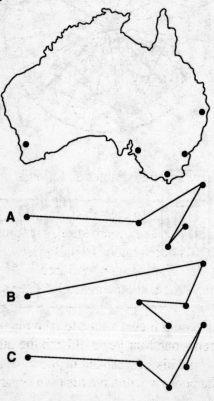

12. Consider pairs of opposite numbers on the dartboard shown below. Subtract the sum of the five lowest pairs from the sum of the five highest pairs.

13. A holiday brochure quotes as follows:

14 days £210
Long stay £62 per week after first fortnight
Children under 10 half price
Children under 5 free
Single room supplement £1.50 per day

How much would it cost a man to take his wife and two children – one four years old and the other nine years old – and his 17-year-old nephew for six weeks? His nephew will have his own separate room.

14. What is X?

11	4	8	7	6	X	4	1
	0	5	2	1	1	9	

15. All except one of these words have three things in common. Which is the exception?

A. ARCADIA
B. EFFERVESCENCE
C. HASHISH
D. TREATMENT
E. MESMERISM
F. GAUGING

**NOW CHECK YOUR ANSWERS
AND KEEP A NOTE OF YOUR SCORE.**

Answers

1. C **(Score 1 point)**

A must have all diamonds, as C has two hearts. As D finishes with all spades, he must hold the king and queen of spades, exchanging the queen of hearts for the jack of spades (which must be the odd black card held by C).

2. A. light, B. sad, C. starboard, D. hate, E. extrovert, F. fiction, G. winner, H. bad, I. sleeping, J. forte **(Score 1 point if all correct)**

3. F **(Score 1 point)**

All the others start and finish with R. A. Recorder, B. Roller, C. Radiator, D. Ruler, E. Rudder, G. Riser, H. River (Thames) and I. Razor. E. (Rake) starts with R but finishes with E.

4. A **(Score 1 point)**

Pinion A has 12 teeth, so 36 teeth will rotate in three revolutions. Pinion B will rotate clockwise. Although there are intermediate pinions between A and B, which may have led you to believe they would rotate in the same direction, the inner teeth on the very large annular ring will cause pinion B to rotate in the opposite direction to A.

5. $2\frac{2}{3}$ pints **(Score 1 point)**

Each container will then hold $5\frac{1}{3}$ pints – that is: $\frac{1}{3}$ pint to B and $2\frac{1}{3}$ pints to C.

6. K **(Score 1 point)**

A–H–N, B–I–P, C–M–O, D–L–F and E–G–J.

7. X is 2, Y is 1, Z is 3 **(Score 1 point if all correct)**

All rows should add to 20.

8. B **(Score 1 point)**

Consider the Roman numerals: XXXX is XX multiplied by X – that is, 20 multiplied by 10 = 200; ACCENT contains CC (200), XXXXXXX is XXX multiplied by XXX – that is, 30 multiplied by 30 = 900; ACME contains C M (900). XXXXXX is XXX multiplied by XX – that is, 30 multiplied by 20 = 600; REDCAP contains DC (600).

9. SOFTEN (Score 1 point)

The initials of the numbers are the initials of the words: Six – S, One – O, Four – F, Two – T, Eight – E and Nine – N.

10. G (Score 1 point)

All the others start with F: A. Feather, B. Four, C. Face, D. Five, E. Fan, F. Fourteen and H. Fingers.

11. C (Score 1 point)

12. 26 (Score 1 point)

The five highest pairs add to 118; the five lowest pairs add to 92.

13. £1,666 (Score 1 point)

14. 5 (Score 1 point)

The first term is the sum of the last three terms in the bottom row. The second term is the sum of the next last three terms. This procedure is continued throughout, so X is the sum of 0, 1 and 4.

15. E (Score 1 point)

In all the others the first, middle and last letters are the same; in Mesmerism the letter M does not occur in the middle.

REMEMBER TO KEEP A NOTE OF YOUR SCORE.

Notes: In Question 2 the only word that may have defeated you was forte (the opposite of piano). Those who have read my previous books – or those who are mechanically-minded – should have no difficulty with Question 4, although the direction of rotation may have confused you, if you overlooked the fact that the top pinion of the inner three would rotate in the same direction as the inner teeth on the large annular ring. In Question 9 you either spotted immediately that it was simply a matter of using initials or wasted much time in trying to work out a non-existent relationship between the cards and the dominoes.

---

1. These two clocks are erratic time-keepers: clock A loses 15 minutes in every hour, while clock B gains 20 minutes in every hour. In how many hours will they again show an exact hour, and what time will each clock show then?

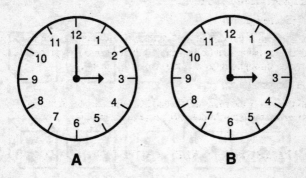

2. Write the letters that will complete three different words. From those letters select four Roman numerals. Add them together and give the total, again in Roman numerals.

E _ I _ E N T

---

3. If GOLD is HOME, CORD is DOSE, BARD is CASE and COME is DONE, what is SONS?

4. What is X?

   3 12 83 130 3 130 313 1303 1 X 31

5. In each row there is one die that does not agree with the other dice in the same row. State the three dice.

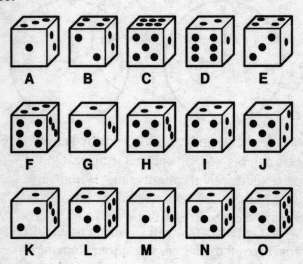

6. Which is the odd one out?
    A. ONAGER   E. CHEAP
    B. RAPE   F. LUMP
    C. CHARIOT   G. MARLED
    D. PRUDE

7. What is X?

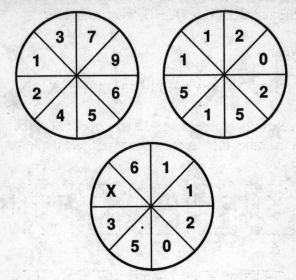

8. Multiply the number that is midway between the lowest number and the one that is nearest to the highest number by the number that is midway between the highest number and the one that is nearest to the lowest number.

39	9	26	49	5
35	51	43	14	41
8	11	7	38	30

9. Which is the odd one out?

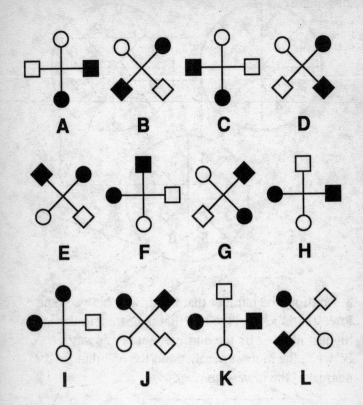

A   B   C   D

E   F   G   H

I   J   K   L

10. Which five of the pieces shown below will form the square?

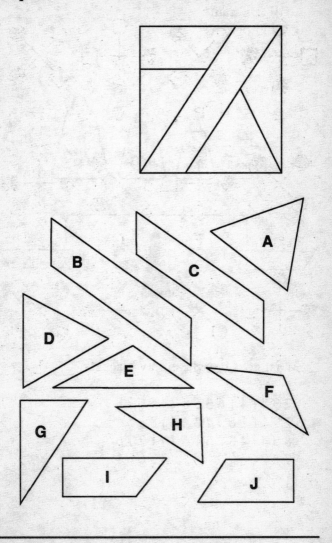

11. How would you arrange the weights on the pans of the scales so that you could weigh the following?
    A. 19 kilograms
    B. 25 kilograms
    C. 31 kilograms

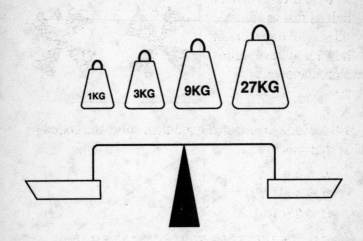

12. What goes into the empty brackets?

1 2 3 4 (4 1 6 3 5 8 7) 5 6 7 8
6 2 7 1 (1 6 3 7 8 4 5) 8 3 5 4
3 8 5 4 (4 3 2 5 1 6 7) 1 2 7 6
4 7 6 2 (   ) 3 6 5 1

13. A revolves at 40 revolutions a minute; B revolves 1½ times as fast as A; C revolves twice as fast as B; and D revolves half as fast as all the others put together. At how many revolutions a minute does D revolve?

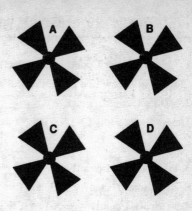

14. Decode the *numbers* and then solve the coded sentence below:

    A. 1 2 3 4 4
    B. 5 4 6 4 7
    C. 4 8 9 10 1

5 8 7 9 1 2 4 6 4 3 5 4 5 8 7 1 2 4 7 8 9 10 1

15. KITTEN is to A as
    CYGNET is to B as
    PARR is to C as
    GOSLING is to D as
    LEVERET is to E
What are A, B, C, D and E?

NOW CHECK YOUR ANSWERS AND KEEP A NOTE OF YOUR SCORE.

Answers

1. 12 hours (**Score 1 point if all correct**)

Clock A will show 12 o'clock; Clock B will show 7 o'clock.

2. MDXV (**Score 1 point**)

The words are EMINENT, EVIDENT and EXIGENT. The Roman numerals in these words are M, V, D and X, that is; 1,000, 5, 500 and 10, which, added together, come to 1,515.

3. TOOT (**Score 1 point**)

Each consonant is moved one place forwards in the alphabet.

4. 30 (**Score 1 point**)

Correctly spaced, the series becomes, 31, 28, 31, 30, 31, 30, 31, 31, 30, 31, 30(X) and 31 – that is, the days in the months of the year.

5. D, J and L (**Score 1 point if all correct**)

In the top row the top face shows the addition of the other two faces; the exception is D. In the middle row the front face shows the addition of the other two faces; the exception is J. In the bottom row the right-hand face shows the addition of the other two faces; the exception is L.

6. C (**Score 1 point**)

This is an anagram of HARICOT. The others are anagrams of fruits: A. ORANGE, B. PEAR, D. DRUPE, E. PEACH, F. PLUM and G. MEDLAR.

7. 8 (**Score 1 point**)

All corresponding sectors add to 10. Starting at 1 in the first circle, the corresponding numbers thereafter are 1 and 8 (X).

8. 783 (**Score 1 point**)

The lowest number is 5; the nearest to the highest number is 49; the midway number between them is 27. The highest number is 51; the nearest to the lowest number is 7; the midway number between them is 29. 27 multiplied by 29 is 783.

9. I (**Score 1 point**)

10. A, B, E, G and J (**Score 1 point if all correct**)

11. A. 27 and 3 kilograms on one side; 1 kilogram on the other side. B. 27 and 1 kilogram on one side; 3 kilograms on the other side. C. 27, 3 and 1 kilogram on either side. **(Score 1 point if all correct)**

12. 2 4 6 6 3 1 5 **(Score 1 point)**

The digits are transposed in the same order throughout, but in each case the second digit on the left outside the brackets is omitted.

13. 110 **(Score 1 point)**

A = 40 rpm, B = 60 rpm and C = 120. A, B and C together revolve at 220 rpm; therefore D revolves at 110 rpm

14. A. THREE, B. SEVEN and C. EIGHT. Sing the verses in the night **(Score 1 point if all correct)**

15. A. CAT, B. SWAN, C. SALMON, D. GOOSE and E. HARE **(Score 1 point if all correct)**

REMEMBER TO KEEP A NOTE OF YOUR SCORE.

Notes: In previous books I warned you to watch for series that were incorrectly spaced and that usually become quite obvious when spaced correctly. Question 4 was a good example of this. In Question 12 the transposition of the digits, a ploy you have probably encountered before, was complicated by the omission of one of the digits. In Question 14 the decoding of the numbers was fairly easy, since A had to be THREE (ending in a double letter), from which B and C became clear. The fact that the word 'numbers' was printed in italics gave a hint to what you were looking for. Having decoded the numbers, the message presented little difficulty.

NOW TOTAL YOUR SCORES FOR THE THREE TESTS IN THIS SECTION AND COMPARE THEM WITH THE RATINGS THAT FOLLOW.

Ratings in Group III

Test 1 – Average 9 points
Test 2 – Average 7 points
Test 3 – Average 6 points

Out of a possible 47

Over 35	Excellent
30–35	Very good
23–29	Good
22	Average
15–21	Fair
Under 15	Poor

Now work out your total score for all the tests and find your overall rating from the scores on the next page.

Overall Ratings for All the Tests

The total number of possible points is 153, and the average score throughout is 68: Group I-27; Group II-19; Group III-22.

Over 113 – Excellent
90–112 – Very good
69-89 – Good
68 – Average
50-67 – Fair
Under 50 – Poor

As I mentioned in the Introduction, this book makes no claims to assigning an IQ level to your results. Although it will be a source of personal satisfaction if you scored an over-average rating, do not despair if your rating was poor. As happened with pre-testing in my previous books, the overall average is under 50 per cent, and I do not deny that some of the problems were very difficult, especially within the stringent time limits that were imposed.

I hope that these problems have given you pleasure as well as some enlightenment, and that they will provide a firm foundation for any tests of a similar nature that you may have to take one day – not just for pleasure, but because something more important can depend on the outcome.